The Little Book of

MUSIC
THEORY

Wise Publications
London/New York/Sydney/Paris/Copenhagen/Madrid/Tokyo

Exclusive distributors:
Music Sales Limited
8/9 Frith Street, London W1V 5TZ, England.
Music Sales Pty Limited
120 Rothschild Avenue
Rosebery, NSW 2018, Australia.

Order No.AM954855
ISBN 0-7119-7824-7
This book © Copyright 1999 by Wise Publications

Book engraved and designed by Digital Music Art

Cover design by Trickett & Webb

Printed in the United Kingdom by
Printwise Limited, Haverhill, Suffolk.

Your Guarantee of Quality
As publishers, we strive to produce every book to the highest commercial
standards. Particular care has been given to specifying acid-free, neutral-sized paper
made from pulps which have not been elemental chlorine bleached. This pulp is from
farmed sustainable forests and was produced with special regard for the environment.
Throughout, the printing and binding have been planned to ensure a sturdy,
attractive publication which should give years of enjoyment.
If your copy fails to meet our high standards, please inform us and we will gladly replace it.

Music Sales' complete catalogue describes thousands of titles and is
available in full colour sections by subject, direct from Music Sales Limited.
Please state your areas of interest and send a cheque/postal order for £1.50 for postage to:
Music Sales Limited, Newmarket Road, Bury St. Edmunds, Suffolk IP33 3YB.

www.musicsales.com

CONTENTS

INTRODUCTION

Have you ever wanted to understand more about music, or write your own?

The Little Book Of Music Theory will give you an introduction to the language of music and help you understand its essential simplicity. So if you have ever been curious about how music works, this is the book for you. The concepts explained here are common to all Western music, be it classical or pop, rock or folk, blues or soul. If you've ever wanted to write your own music, an understanding of these fundamental concepts will help.

Once, only writers on classical music talked about musical theory. Now, increasingly, books on popular music are using some of its ideas and terms. Whether you're a singer or an instrumentalist, a member of a string quartet or a rock band, or just someone who loves listening to music, knowing a little theory will enhance your awareness and increase the pleasure music gives you.

This book is supplemented by The Little Book of Musical Terms, a mini music dictionary containing all the definitions you need for both classical and contemporary music styles. See p64 for details.

1.   THE BASICS

Centuries ago, long before the invention of any recording technology, people played and created music. They needed a way of preserving it and teaching it to other musicians. The question was, how? The answer: invent a diagram.

The Stave

The result was the stave, five lines where notes are placed on or between the lines, lower or higher according to their pitch.

Stave

The Treble Clef

To fix the pitch of the lines, we use a clef (from the French, meaning 'key'). The treble clef is a squiggly shape beginning on the second line of the stave. This fixes the position of that line, as the note G. The treble clef is also sometimes known as the G clef.

Treble Clef

Letter Names

There are seven note letter names in music: ABCDEFG. There is nothing magical about letter names; any convenient shorthand symbol could have been used, including numbers. These are the so-called 'white notes' of the keyboard, and the sequence ABCDEFG is repeated over and over, from low notes to high.

The lines of the treble clef stave mark the notes E G B D F. Here's an easy way to remember this - think of the phrase Every Good Boy Deserves Fun. The spaces within the stave spell the word FACE. The space immediately below the stave is D and the space above is G.

Different Clefs

It is possible to have other clefs which change the meaning of the stave's lines. Apart from the treble clef the most common is the bass or F clef. This is most commonly used for the left hand of a piano part, and low-pitched instruments such as bass guitar.

The clef starts on the fourth line up, fixing the position of the note F. The lines now spell out G B D F A, the spaces A C E G.

Leger Lines

If we need notes higher or lower than this we can use what are called *leger* lines. These are little lines which can be placed above or below the stave, for notes whose pitch is too high or low for the stave.

Several leger lines can be attached to a note, but obviously the more you use the harder it is for the eye to take in at a glance exactly how many there are. So if a piece of music involves a long succession of high leger notes the symbol '8ve' can be placed above the stave and the notes written one octave lower then they sound. This removes the leger lines and makes the music easier to read.

Transposing Instruments

Certain instruments are by convention not written at exactly the pitch at which they sound. This is because their range, written at the strict pitch, would take them too much above or below a stave. This would mean often using leger lines and a headache for the musician! Such instruments are called transposing instruments. The notes they play actually sound at a different pitch to the same note played by a non-transposing instrument (such as a piano). Usually music for these instruments is written in a different key, to enable musicians to play the same piece of music together.

Middle C

The term Middle C is commonly used by musicians as a reference point to distinguish one note from another. As there are lots of C's (and other notes) all the way along the keyboard, and in other instruments, we have to be able to distinguish between them. The note Middle C has a frequency of 256Hz - basically, it is the C nearest to the middle of a keyboard or piano.

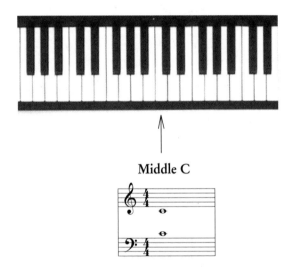

Middle C

Middle C is written on the first leger line below the treble clef or on the first leger line above the bass clef. This is still the same note but the treble and bass clefs are separated in order to make notes easier to read, and to distinguish between the left and right hands on the keyboard.

The music for many instruments can be written on one clef – the piano is an exception because it has a very wide range of notes from low to high. Consequently, its music needs a bass clef (for the left hand) and a treble clef (for the right hand). The two staves are joined by a bracket (see below).

Tablature

In recent years another type of diagram has been popularised for the guitar, which looks like this:

The six lines represent the actual strings of the guitar, unlike the stave which is a symbolic representation. Tablature, or TAB as it is abbreviated, is not a modern invention – in fact a similar form was used as far back as the 16th Century, for instruments such as the lute.

Instead of writing notes on the lines, fret numbers are written, so that the player sees immediately which fret to play on which string. This takes out one step in the reading process. With a conventional stave the player has to recognise what note is required, then decide where to play it. The disadvantage of tablature is that it does not give an indication of rhythm, so usually it is combined with a traditional stave to give a fuller picture of the music.

Unlike the piano, stringed instruments such as the guitar usually allow you to play the same note in more than one place. A player can choose where to play the note, and which fingering to use.

Here is an example of tablature for the bass guitar:

… and guitar tablature combined with the stave.

Here's a handy reference guide to some of the most common notations in TAB:

THE MUSICAL STAVE shows pitches and rhythms and is divided by lines into bars. Pitches are named after the first seven letters of the alphabet.

TABLATURE graphically represents the guitar fingerboard. Each horizontal line represents a string, and each number represents a fret.

4th string, 2nd fret   1st & 2nd strings open, played together   open D chord

---

SEMI-TONE BEND: Strike the note and bend up a semi-tone (1/2 step).

WHOLE-TONE BEND: Strike the note and bend up a whole-tone (whole step).

GRACE NOTE BEND: Strike the note and bend as indicated. Play the first note as quickly as possible.

QUARTER-TONE BEND: Strike the note and bend up a 1/4 step.

HAMMER-ON: Strike the first (lower) note with one finger, then sound the higher note (on the same string) with another finger by fretting it without picking.

PULL-OFF: Place both fingers on the notes to be sounded. Strike the first note and without picking, pull the finger off to sound the second (lower) note.

BEND & RELEASE: Strike the note and bend up as indicated, then release back to the original note.

LEGATO SLIDE (GLISS): Strike the first note and then slide the same fret-hand finger up or down to the second note. The second note is not struck.

SHIFT SLIDE (GLISS & RESTRIKE): Same as legato slide, except the second note is struck.

2.   ACCIDENTALS

Introduction To Intervals

Between any note and another note there must be an interval or a gap. In music there is a simple system for measuring this.

The smallest interval used in most Western music is called the semi-tone. This is the distance between B and C, or E and F, the two white notes which are next to each other on a piano. All the other notes are a tone apart. This means that half-way (a semi-tone) between A and B is another note. We can think of this as either A plus a semi-tone (A sharp), or B minus a semi-tone (B flat).

Sharps, Flats and Naturals

A sharp sign (♯) raises the pitch of any note by a semitone. A flat sign (♭) lowers the pitch of any note by a semitone. So A♯ and B♭ are the same note and on the piano are played by the same black key.

These signs are called accidentals. There is a further sign called a *natural* (♮) which cancels out the effect of a sharp or a flat. In rare instances a note is sometimes raised or lowered by a whole tone. This can result in a *double sharp* (×) or a *double flat* (♭♭). Thus A× is actually the same note as B, but it may be necessary to preserve the rule that every letter must be present in a scale or key.

By introducing the five sharp/flat notes (sometimes called black notes) to our original seven we produce a sequence that looks like this:

A A♯/B♭ B C C♯/D♭ D D♯/E♭ E F F♯/G♭ G G♯/A♭

Amazingly, all of our music is created out of just these 12 notes!

Octaves

We mentioned before that there are several 'copies' or 'versions' of each note on the keyboard. For instance, the note called A can occur up to 8 times on a full-sized piano. That's because these A's are at different pitches, but sound similar due to their wavelengths and cycles per second. Every 12 semitones, (an octave) the wavelength either doubles (going up the keyboard) or halves (going down).

The best way to understand this is to locate several different versions, or octaves, of one note (eg. A), and play them, listening for the differences between them.

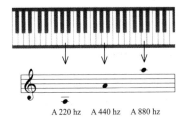

A 220 hz   A 440 hz   A 880 hz

3. RHYTHM

So far we've established how to represent the pitch of a note. But how do we indicate how long it should last, and what speed to play it?

Every note in a melody lasts a certain length - it has duration and rhythm. To represent this each note has a certain symbol, which is placed on the stave in relation to the other notes around it, at the appropriate pitch. This then tells us everything we need to know about the length and speed of the note.

Here's a quick-reference guide to each note:

Symbol	Name	US equivalent	no. of beats
o	semi-breve	whole note	4
♩	minim	half note	2
♩	crotchet	quarter note	1
♪	quaver	eighth note	$1/2$
♪	semi-quaver	sixteenth note	$1/4$
♪	demi-semi-quaver	thirty-second note	$1/8$
♪	hemi-demi-semiquaver	sixty-fourth note	$1/16$

Here's what the notes look like placed on a stave. Tails can go up or down depending on various conventions such as which line they are placed on (notes above the middle line tend to have their tails drawn downward) or how many parts are represented at once on a single stave.

More complicated rhythms

Rhythms can be more complicated or subtle than we could write down using just these symbols. To be able to represent other rhythms and note lengths we need a few more symbols.

Dots

A dot placed after a note increases the duration of that note by 50%. Dots can only be used within a bar; they do not span bars. Here are some examples.

| 3 | = | 2 | + | 1 | 1½ | = | 1 | + | ½ | ¾ | = | ½ | + | ¼ |

Ties

A tie joins two notes together. Only the first note is played, the duration of the second one is added on to the first (see below). This enables a note to last for more than one bar, or several beats plus a fraction of a beat. Dotted notes can also be tied to each other.

Rest

A rest is an indication of silence. This could be for part of a beat, a beat, a whole bar or many bars at a stretch. Each note has its own type of rest. Here they are in matched pairs.

Dotted Rest

A rest can also have a dot placed with it which adds 50% silence to the original length of silence. Here's an example:

1½ beat rest

Beams

As with the stave, certain conventions about the way music is printed have been created to make things easier for the eye. When there are a number of quavers or semi-quavers in a bar they are usually grouped together, using 'beams' to make them easier to read.

Have a look at this example:

Here it is again written out properly:

It's much easier to see the rhythm patterns now that the notes are grouped.

It is important to remember that musical notation - both rhythm and pitch - is to some extent approximate. The subtleties of pitch and timing in a singer's voice cannot always be exactly put down on paper, and the more precise a system of notation is, the harder it is to read. Standard musical notation is a good compromise between the extremes of simplicity and precision.

Tempo

In past times the speed (tempo) of a piece of music was indicated by Italian terms such as 'largo', 'moderato', 'andante', 'allegro' and so on. The interpretation of such terms as 'slowly', 'moderately' or 'lively' is to a certain degree subjective. A more precise method can be found at the start of most recent sheet music. You'll find a note, usually a crotchet (signifying the beat) and a number:

♩ = **120**

This is the BPM - beats per minute. If you have a metronome or drum machine this figure tells you the exact speed of the music.

Time Signature

Whatever the tempo, and whatever the rhythm patterns found in each bar, almost all music has a constant beat. When you dance to music or tap your foot or drum your fingers on a table, you're responding to the beat. This is governed by the time signature - a way of organising the overall rhythm of the music. The note symbols given in the table above are given specific meaning by the tempo of the music and the time signature itself. On their own they don't really mean anything.

A time signature is found at the beginning of a piece of music. It consists of two numbers, like this:

Common Time

The top number refers to the number of beats in the bar, and the bottom number indicates which type of note makes up the beat. The most common time-signature is ¼, which basically means there are 4 crotchet, or quarter-note, beats in each bar. This is written in two ways (C standing for 'common time'):

Example:

How Many Notes In A Bar?

A bar of ¼ can use any number or mixture of notes and rests provided that the total number of notes and/or rests do not exceed four crotchet beats.

The following example shows how many different patterns of notes add up to four beats.

The following two bars show examples of too many beats in a each bar. These bars are impossible in ⁴⁄₄ time.

| 3 | + | ½ + ½ + 1 | | 1 + 2 | + | ½ + ½ + 1½ |

= 5 beats   = 5 ½ beats

Simple Time

Other common time signatures include ³⁄₄ (waltz time), ²⁄₄ , and, less commonly, time signatures that use a minim, or half-note, as the beat, such as ⁴⁄₂ , ³⁄₂ or ²⁄₂ .

Occasionally you'll find bars of ⁶⁄₄ , or even the asymmetrical ⁵⁄₄ (as in Dave Brubeck's popular jazz classic 'Take Five').

All of these time signatures are known as 'simple time', as each beat in the bar, crotchet, or minim, can be subdivided into two or four.

Compound Time

Fortunately, this doesn't mean time spent in prison! As well as having time-signatures which can be divided into two, there are also time signatures based on dotted notes where the beat divides into three.

$\frac{6}{8}$ is one such time-signature. There are six eighth notes (quavers) in a bar, however, they are grouped into two pairs of three, making a substantial difference to the sound of the bar, and the emphasis on the beat. Compare it with $\frac{3}{4}$ which has the same number of quavers (six) but three audible beats, since the quavers are grouped into three pairs of two.

Here's an example of $\frac{6}{8}$. The first bar shows the characteristic two groups of three quavers.

The first bar of this example of $\frac{3}{4}$ time demonstrates the difference in quaver groupings between $\frac{3}{4}$ and $\frac{6}{8}$ (above).

We can make the same comparison between $\frac{12}{8}$ and $\frac{4}{4}$. Both have four beats. In $\frac{4}{4}$ there are eight quavers, but in $\frac{12}{8}$ there are twelve, grouped into four groups of three. $\frac{9}{8}$ has three beats each of which divide into three. Compound time signatures such as these have a distinctive rhythm or 'bounce'. $\frac{12}{8}$ for example is popular for blues songs:

Unusual Time Signatures

It is also possible to have odd-numbered signatures such as $\frac{5}{8}$, $\frac{7}{8}$, or $\frac{11}{8}$. These can be disconcerting because they tend to sound like $\frac{6}{8}$, $\frac{4}{4}$ or $\frac{12}{8}$ - but with one quaver missing. The rhythmic consequence of this foreshortening is that the beginning of the next bar always comes half a beat earlier than you initially anticipate - a factor which keeps audiences and performers on their toes!

Triplets

It is also possible to split a beat in simple time into three. This is called a triplet. Half, quarter, eighth or sixteenth notes can all be turned into triplets in this way. The triplet allows for a temporary change of rhythm which doesn't continue long enough to need a change of time signature.

4.   MAJOR KEYS

The basis of almost all music is a scale of some kind.
A scale is a sequence of notes relating to a key, with a fixed pattern of gaps between each note.

The most important scale in Western music is the major scale. It is a way of dividing an octave into seven notes. Its pattern is made up of: tone - tone - semitone - tone - tone - tone - semitone.

Here's what happens if we start on C:

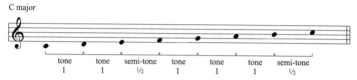

The gaps happen to be exactly where we need them and the two semitone gaps are in the right place – so there are no sharps or flats needed to make this scale fit the pattern of tones/ semitones. It can be played entirely on the white notes of the keyboard.

If we try the same thing on G something different occurs:

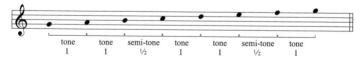

The first semitone is in the right place, but the second isn't - it has fallen between notes 6 and 7, instead of between 7 and 8. We have to make an adjustment, which is to sharpen the F to F♯. This makes the semitone between notes 6 and 7 increase to a tone, and also halves the gap between 7 and 8 - which is what we need:

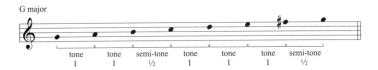

When a musician plays in the key of G major all the Fs are played sharp.

Now let's try starting on an F:

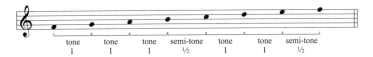

Now we have the opposite problem: the final semitone gap is correct, but the earlier one which should be between 3 and 4 is in the wrong place - between 4 and 5. The gap between 3 and 4 is only supposed to be a semitone but here it's a tone. To make it smaller, we have to flatten the B to B♭:

This gives us the scale of F major.

When a musician plays in the key of F major all the B's are played flat. This raises the question – why not use a sharp like this:

F major

tone 1   tone 1   semi-tone ½   tone 1   tone 1   tone 1   semi-tone ½

We could do this - but conventionally, every letter name must be present in a scale. So here, instead of B, there are two A's. That's why we have to call A♯ a B♭ and think of it as the fourth note flattened, not the third note sharpened.

The Sharp Major Keys

It is possible to build a major scale from any of the 12 notes. With the exception of C major which has no key signature, major scales use either sharps or flats. They never mix them. Here are the major scales of the keys which use sharps, in sequence:

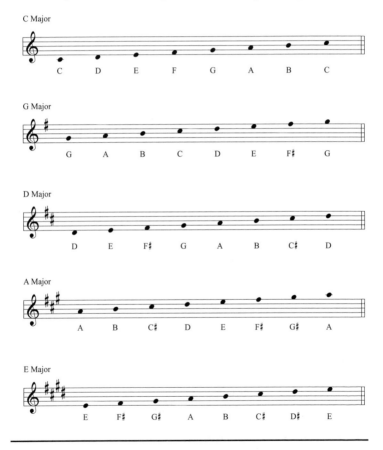

Here are a few tips to help you remember the progression of the sharp major scales.

> • The new additional sharp always appears on the 7th note.
>
> • All the sharps in a scale are carried over and automatically become part of the next until all the notes are sharpened.
>
> • The starting notes proceed by the interval of a fifth (see p37): C G D A E B F♯ C♯.

The key signature always appears at the start of a piece of music and tells you which sharps or flats to play throughout the piece (unless there are accidentals or key changes). The music would look very messy if the four sharps needed for E major were printed in every bar!

The Flat Major Keys

Here are the scales of the major keys which use flats, in sequence:

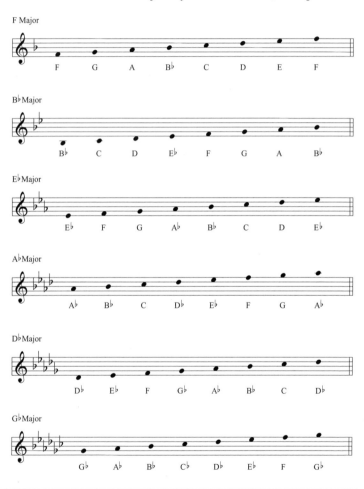

C♭ Major

C♭ D♭ E♭ F♭ G♭ A♭ B♭ C♭

Here are some tips on the flat major keys:

•The new additional flat always appears on the 4th note.

•All the flats in a scale are carried over and automatically become part of the next until all the notes are flattened.

•The starting notes proceed by an interval of a fourth: after C F B♭ E♭ A♭ D♭ G♭ C♭.

If there are only 12 notes, how is it that there are 15 major scales?

The answer is that three are actually the same, but have two different names: D♭ = C♯, G♭ = F♯, and C♭ = B. The reason for this is to simplify the notation and reading of a piece of music.

A piece of music can begin in one key, change to other keys, and perhaps finish in the original key. Changing key is called *modulation*. Key-changing is vital to longer pieces, avoiding monotony and creating the sense of a musical journey.

5.   MINOR KEYS

There are other ways of dividing up the octave. In contrast to major scales, minor scales have a sad quality to them. Whereas there is only one type of major scale (tone, tone, semitone, tone, tone, tone, semitone) there are three forms of minor scale.

The Harmonic Minor

The harmonic minor scale has an 'angular' sound, due to the different placement of the tones and semitones within it. Have a look at the scale below (A harmonic minor):

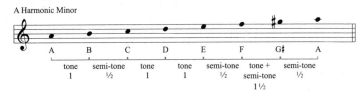

A Harmonic Minor

This scale is found more in classical music than in popular music, although rock guitarists sometimes use it when they want to produce an exotic, non-Western sound by playing the last four notes and adding bends to them.

The Melodic Minor

The harmonic minor is not an easy scale for singers. The melodic minor is a variation which smoothes out this gap, which can be awkward, especially for singers. Here's A melodic minor:

A Melodic Minor

A B C D E F♯ G♯ A G♮ F♮ E D C B A

It has the unusual characteristic of using different notes going up, to going down. Ascending, the 6th note is also sharpened, thus removing the large gap between 6 and 7 found in the harmonic minor. Descending, the notes are restored to their natural form.

The Natural Minor

The third type of minor scale is this:

A Melodic Minor

A B C D E F G A

This is called the natural minor scale. It is found in folk music, some classical music of the C19th and early 20th, and frequently in many types of popular music. It is also known as the Aeolian mode. We will talk about the scales known as modes a little later.

The Sharp Minor Keys

Each major key has a 'relative minor' which essentially shares the same key signature. The root note of this relative minor is always a minor third (1½ tones) below the major key root note. If you are using the natural minor scale, no additional accidentals will crop up in the music. If the harmonic minor scale is used, one additional accidental will appear in the music which would not be present in the major key. Here are the minor keys which add a sharp to the seventh note:

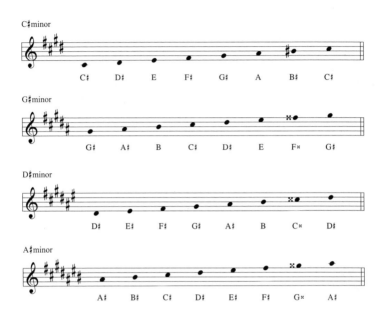

The Flat Minor Keys

Here are the scales of the minor keys with flats in the key signature:

The Flat Minor Keys (cont.)

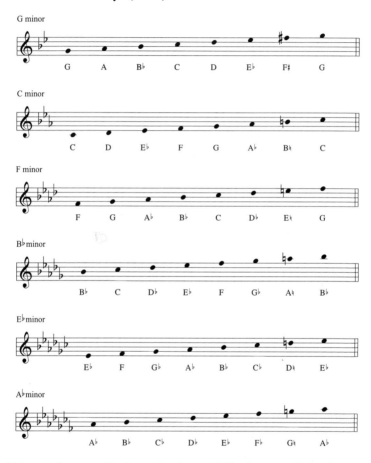

Although these are flat keys, D minor and G minor use sharps for the seventh note, as it is an accidental (not part of the key signature), and also so that every note name can be represented.

6.   INTERVALS

As we mentioned earlier (see Chapter 2), an interval is simply the distance between two notes.

The term *diatonic* refers to any interval occurring within the major scale. E.g: a major third = a distance of 2½ tones between the two notes.

If an interval is greater than an octave, it can be described as a ninth, tenth, eleventh etc. These are known as *compound* intervals.

Note that when intervals are turned upside-down they turn into the following:

minor 2nd	=	major 7th
major 2nd	=	minor 7th
minor 3rd	=	major 6th
major 3rd	=	minor 6th
perfect 4th	=	perfect 5th
augmented 4th	=	diminished 5th

Over the page is a diagram to measure the distance – or interval – between the notes within one octave. It is referenced against the scale of C, but to find these intervals in another key, simply count up (in tones/semitones) from the root note.

Interval Guide

Name of interval	Distance between notes (in tones)	Degree of scale (in C major)
unison	0	C - C *
minor 2nd	½	C - D♭
major 2nd	1	C - D
minor 3rd	1½	C - E♭
major 3rd	2	C - E
perfect 4th	2½	C - F
augmented 4th	3	C - F♯
diminished 5th	3	C - G♭
perfect 5th	3½	C - G
augmented 5th	4	C - G♯
minor 6th	4	C - A♭
major 6th	4½	C - A
minor 7th	5	C - B♭
major 7th	5½	C - B
perfect octave	6	C - C **

*only possible on stringed instruments, where the same note can be played in two different places.

** the distance between one note and the same note an octave higher.

Certain intervals are more commonly used than others. In rock music, the perfect fifth is frequently used in rhythm guitar playing (power-chords). Heavy rock riffs often use perfect fifths and fourths singly or in combination. Jazz guitarists like using octaves to thicken single-note melody lines whereas thirds and sixths are the intervals most commonly used in vocal harmonies.

Here are some intervals, with the bottom note as C:

7. MODES

So far we have looked at the major scale, and the natural, harmonic and melodic minor scales. The major scale and the natural minor were both known to the ancient Greeks. They called the major scale the Ionian mode and the natural minor the Aeolian mode. There were five other modes, which are occasionally used in popular music today.

The Dorian Mode

The Dorian mode is the pattern of intervals found in the sequence D - D on the white notes of the keyboard.

Dorian mode

D E F G A B C D

If this is compared with D natural minor –

D natural minor

D E F G A B♭ C D

– you can see that one note is different, B instead of B♭. So the Dorian mode can be thought of as the natural minor with a sharpened 6th.

The dorian scale sounds edgier than the natural minor and is favoured by bands like Santana.

The Phrygian Mode

The Phrygian mode is the pattern of intervals found in the sequence E - E on the white notes of the keyboard.

If this is compared with E natural minor –

– you can see that one note is different, F instead of F♯. So the Phrygian mode can be thought of as the natural minor with a flattened second. It also has a distinctly Spanish flavour.

The Lydian Mode

The Lydian mode is the pattern of intervals found in the sequence F - F on the white notes of the keyboard.

If this is compared with F major –

– you can see that one note is different, B instead of B♭. So the Lydian mode can be thought of as the major with a sharpened 4th.

The Mixolydian Mode

The Mixolydian mode is the pattern of intervals found in the sequence G - G on the white notes of the piano.

If this is compared with G major –

– you can see that one note is different, F instead of F♯. So the Mixolydian mode can be thought of as the major scale with a flattened 7th.

Since much pop and rock is blues-influenced, and since blues often flattens the seventh of the scale, the mixolydian is the most common of these five modes.

The Locrian Mode

The Locrian mode is the pattern of intervals found in the sequence B - B on the white notes of the piano.

If this is compared with B natural minor –

– you can see that two notes have been changed, C instead of C♯, and F instead of F♯. So the Locrian mode can be thought of as the natural minor with a flattened 2nd and 5th. This means that the Locrian scale is the furthest from the normal major or minor scale and is therefore quite uncommon.

Transposing Modes

Any mode can be transposed onto any note. It is possible to have a C dorian, C phrygian, C lydian, C mixolydian or C locrian scale. Accidentals may need to be used to make the gaps between the notes match those between the notes of the mode as indicated before.

Here's an example of the Dorian scale, in C:

Some Other Scales

There are many other types of scale used in different cultures around the world. Here's a quick look at some scales used commonly in rock, pop and blues.

Pentatonic Scale

There are two main types of pentatonic scale. The pentatonic major is merely an edited form of the major scale using 1, 2, 3, 5 and 6.

Here's an example in G:

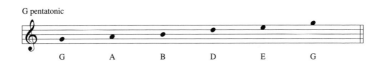

Minor Pentatonic Scale

The pentatonic minor is an edited form of the natural minor scale using 1, 3, 4, 5, and 7.

G minor pentatonic

G   B♭   C   D   F   G

Minor 6th Pentatonic Scale

Here's another interesting sound – take away the 7th and add the natural 6th to the minor pentatonic to create the minor 6th pentatonic.

G minor 6 pentatonic

G   B♭   C   D   E   G

'Blues' Scale

Finally, here's what's known as the 'Blues' scale: a sort of pentatonic minor scale with an added sharpened fourth. Check out the sound of this - some blues players never use anything else!

G Blues scale

G   B♭   C   C♯   D   F   G

8. CHORDS

Music consists of melody, rhythm and harmony – and harmony depends on chords. The next thing we need to look at is how a chord is formed.

What is a chord?

A chord involves three different notes and is also known as a triad. In making a triad the distance between the 1st and middle note, and between the middle and top note, must be an interval of a major or minor third (major third = 2 tones, minor third = 1½ tones.)

Here are the four triad types:

Major triad	C	E	G
intervals		2	1½
Minor triad	C	E♭	G
intervals		1½	2
Augmented triad	C	E	G♯
intervals		2	2
Diminished triad	C	E♭	G♭
intervals		1½	1½

C major   C minor   C augmented   C diminished

The interval gaps are reversed between major and minor. Notice that while the root note and fifth remain the same, the only difference between a major chord and a minor is the note in the middle, the 'third' of the chord. These triads can be formed on any of the 12 notes.

These four triad types have different qualities, and this is one of the reasons music is able to evoke complex feelings. For example, the minor triad seems sad in comparison to the major. Most songs use a combination of major and minor chords.

The augmented and diminished chords are used occasionally, in certain specific contexts. A diminished chord has interval gaps of two minor thirds which makes it closer to the minor than the major - whereas the augmented triad has interval gaps of two major thirds, which makes it closer to the major.

Voicings

If we take the notes of the C major and C minor triads and write them on the stave you can see that many different combinations of the three notes are possible. These variations are called voicings, and modify the effect of the chord.

Inversions

The sound of a chord is also affected by which note is lowest. All of the above examples used C (or the root note) as the lowest note. This is what is known as a *root position* chord.

Consider the next examples.

1st   1st   2nd   2nd

If the third of the chord (E for C major, E♭ for C minor) is placed at the bottom of the chord, we create a *first inversion* – meaning simply to 'turn upside down'. If the fifth of the chord is placed at the bottom, we have created a *second inversion*.

With a simple triad, only the root, first and second inversions are possible. If the chord has four notes in it then it would be possible to have a third inversion – and so on. The number of inversions is always one less than the number of notes in the chord.

Relating Chords To Keys - Major

The chords that belong to a major or minor key are derived from its scale. Let's investigate. Here's the scale of C major with the notes of the scale numbered:

By taking the 1st, 3rd and 5th notes of the scale, we get a triad of C major, C E G. If we then do the same thing with D, using the same notes of the scale, we get D F A, the chord of D minor. By doing the same thing on every note of the scale we form the seven primary chords of the key:

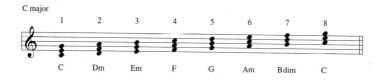

Here are the chords of A major.

And here are the primary chords in E♭ major.

We can use a sort of shorthand to talk about each of these seven chords regardless of which key we happen to be in. We can call the chords by the degrees of the scale in roman numerals - chords I, II, III, IV, V, VI and VII. As all major scales have the same internal musical relationships the sequence of chords always follows the pattern:

major   minor   minor   major   major   minor   diminished

Minor Key Chords

The formation of the chords in a minor key depends on which minor scale we use. Let's take the natural minor scale first.

The Natural Minor

In each case the primary seven chords follow this pattern:

minor   diminished   major   minor   minor   major   major

Here are the primary chords in A natural minor.

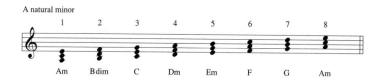

Here are the primary chords in F♯ natural minor.

Here are the primary chords in C natural minor.

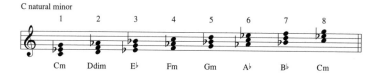

The Harmonic Minor

If, however, we use the harmonic minor form we get a slightly different result. In each case the primary seven chords follow this pattern:

minor   diminished   augmented   minor   major   major   diminished

This different pattern has been caused by the sharpened seventh note, in the harmonic minor scale. Here are some examples:

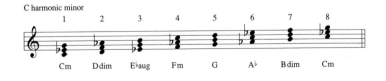

Beyond Major And Minor

So far we have just looked at simple major and minor triads. More complex chords can be built by simply adding more notes to the triad, or altering the top note (the fifth).

Sevenths

Here's one way of altering, or adding to, the basic 3 note triad. By adding the seventh note in the scale, we create a 7th chord.

If we did this with the first six chords in the major scale we would end up with a sequence like this:

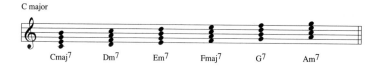

There are three types of chord here: let's look at these.

Dominant Seventh   C E G B♭   1 3 5 ♭7

The most common type of these three chords is the dominant seventh. To form the dominant seventh simply flatten the seventh note of the scale and add it to the triad. It naturally occurs only on the fifth (dominant) note of the major scale and has a tougher sound than the major seventh.

In blues and blues-influenced music where flattened notes are introduced into the harmony, the dominant seventh chord is frequently built on chords I, IV or V.

Major Seventh   C E G B   1 3 5 7

The major seventh naturally occurs in the first and fourth notes of the major scale. It has a rich, expressive sound.

Minor Seventh   C E♭ G B♭   1 ♭3 5 ♭7

The minor seventh naturally occurs on the second, third and sixth notes of the major scale. It has a melancholy sound but is softer than a straight minor chord.

Suspended Chords

Here's another way of altering the sound of basic triads. Suspended chords (sus2 and sus4) are formed by taking away the third degree of the scale – so the chord is neither major or minor– and adding the fourth or second, to create a 'suspension' in the harmony. They are commonly 'resolved' to either a major or minor chord, depending on the key of the piece.

First Octave Chords

Here are the most common types of chord formed by just using a single octave major scale:

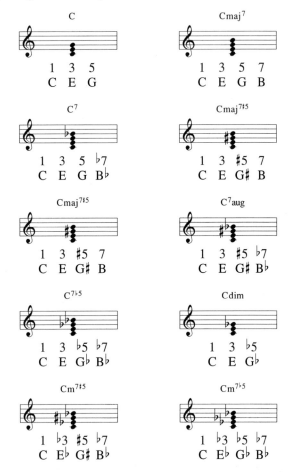

First Octave Chords (cont.)

Cm$^{\flat 6}$

1	$\flat$3	5	$\flat$6
C	E$\flat$	G	A$\flat$

Cm^6

1	$\flat$3	5	6
C	E$\flat$	G	A

Caug

1	3	$\sharp$5
C	E	G$\sharp$

Cdim^7

1	$\flat$3	$\flat$5	$\flat\flat$7
C	E$\flat$	G$\flat$	B$\flat\flat$

C^6

1	3	5	6
C	E	G	A

Csus^2

1	2	5
C	D	G

Csus^4

1	4	5
C	F	G

Cm

1	$\flat$3	5
C	E$\flat$	G

Cm^7

1	$\flat$3	5	$\flat$7
C	E$\flat$	G	B$\flat$

Cm(maj^7)

1	$\flat$3	5	7
C	E$\flat$	G	B

To form more complex chords we can extend the scale to a second octave:

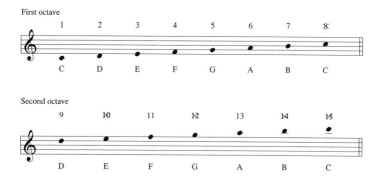

Of these notes only the 9th, 11 and 13th are meaningful - the 8th, 10th, 12th and 15th notes are simply notes of the basic major triad, an octave higher. They don't 'stand out' or alter the sound of the chord in the same way as a 9th or 11th. The 14th is also irrelevant, as the 7th is used instead.

Second Octave Chords

Here are some examples of second octave chords. All of these are reproducible on the piano, but some can only be approximated on the guitar. A correct 13th chord has seven different notes in it - a guitar only has six strings. Your technique has to be magical to get round that!

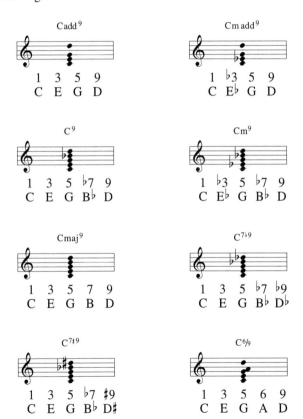

Second Octave Chords (cont.)

Cm^{11}

1	♭3	5	♭7	9	11
C	E♭	G	B♭	D	F

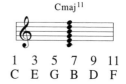

$Cmaj^{11}$

1	3	5	7	9	11
C	E	G	B	D	F

C^{11}

1	3	5	♭7	9	11
C	E	G	B♭	D	F

$C^{7}add^{11}$

1	3	5	♭7	11
C	E	G	B♭	F

C^{13}

1	3	5	♭7	9	11	13
C	E	G	B♭	D	F	A

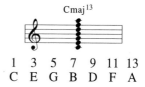

$Cmaj^{13}$

1	3	5	7	9	11	13
C	E	G	B	D	F	A

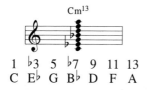

Cm^{13}

1	♭3	5	♭7	9	11	13
C	E♭	G	B♭	D	F	A

$C^{7}add^{13}$

1	3	5	7	13
C	E♭	G	B♭	A

Index

Index

Index

Further Reading

Check out some of the other books in this new series, listed below. These, and many other great titles, are available from all good music retailers, or in case of difficulty, from the Music Sales catalogue, or click on our website: **musicsales.co.uk**.

The Little Book of Musical Terms
AM954866

A bite-size musical dictionary including definitions for both classical and contemporary music styles, notation and theory, instruments - from viol to modern electric guitar, and recording and music business terms. The perfect size for your music case!

The Little Book of Tips and Tricks (for Guitar)
AM954767

This book has everything you need to know to improve your guitar technique, instantly! Sections on equipment, playing rhythm, how to solo, and how to play like the pros!

The Little Book of Chords (for Guitar)
AM954778

A bite-size chord book with fully-illustrated chord diagrams and photos for hundreds of useful chords, including triads, major and minor chords, slash chords, power-chords, sevenths/ninths, sus chords and many more!

The Little Book of Love Lyrics
AM954822

The lyrics to 35 of your favourite old and new love-songs, including 'Could It Be Magic', 'I Will Always Love You', 'Take My Breath Away' and 'Wonderful Tonight'.

Music Sales Limited Newmarket Road Bury St Edmunds Suffolk IP33 3YB
Tel: 01284 702 600

06/06 (58964)